WHEN GODLY PEOPLE DO UNGODLY THINGS

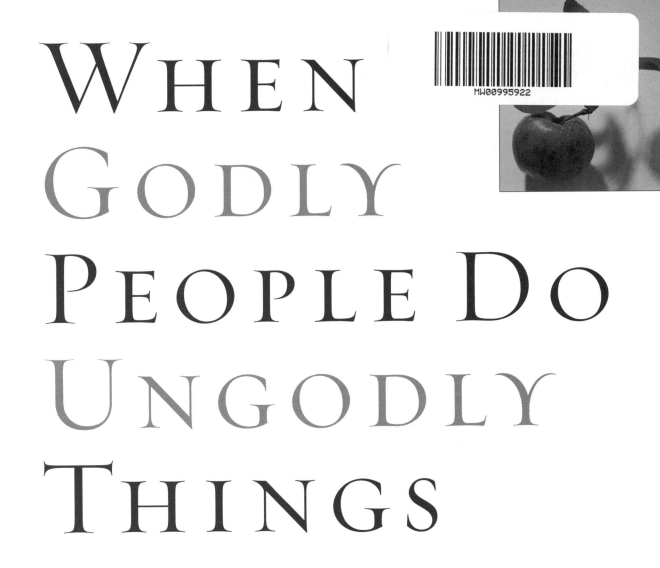

BETH MOORE

LifeWay Press
Nashville, Tennessee

LEADER GUIDE

ISBN 0-6330-9014-X

This book is the text for course CG-0822 in the subject area
Personal Life in the Christian Growth Study Plan.

Dewey Decimal Classification Number: 235.4
Subject Heading: SPIRITUAL WARFARE \ TEMPTATION \ CHRISTIAN LIFE // STUDY AND TEACHING

Editor in Chief: Dale McCleskey
Art Director: Jon Rodda
Editor: Joyce McGregor
Copy Editor: Beth Shive

Cover photo: Howard Bjornson/Photonica
Inside photo, p. 8—Susan Cato

Unless otherwise indicated, Scripture quotations are from the Holy Bible,
New International Version, copyright © 1973, 1978, 1984 by International Bible Society.

Scripture quotations identified The Message are from THE MESSAGE.
Copyright © 1993, 1994, 1995, 1996, 2000, 2001, 2002. Used by permission of NavPress Publishing Group.

Scripture quotations identified KJV are from the *King James Version.*

Scripture quotations identified AMP are from *The Amplified New Testament*
© The Lockman Foundation 1954, 1958, 1987. Used by permission.

Scripture quotations identified NASB are from the NEW AMERICAN STANDARD BIBLE,
© Copyright The Lockman Foundation, 1960, 1962, 1963, 1968, 1971, 1972, 1973, 1975, 1977, 1995.
Used by permission.

Scripture quotations identified CEV are from the *Contemporary English Version*
Copyright © 1991, 1992, 1995 American Bible Society. Used by permission.

Scripture quotations identified HCSB are from the *Holman Christian Standard Bible®*
© Copyright 2001 Holman Bible Publishers, Nashville, TN. All rights reserved.

To order additional copies of this resource: WRITE LifeWay Church Resources Customer Service;
One LifeWay Plaza; Nashville, TN 37234-0013; FAX (615) 251-5933;
PHONE (800) 458-2772; EMAIL to *customerservice@lifeway.com;* ORDER ONLINE at *www.lifeway.com;*
or VISIT the LifeWay Christian Store serving you.

Printed in the United States of America

Leadership and Adult Publishing
LifeWay Church Resources
One LifeWay Plaza
Nashville, TN 37234-0175

CONTENTS

INTRODUCTION

When Godly People Do Ungodly Things is a message of warning, protection, and restoration. Our study goal is to determine how whole-hearted, sincere, and purely devoted followers of Christ can be seduced by the enemy. Through the study we will examine ways to seduce-proof our lives so that we are protected from the enemy's schemes. Finally, we will see in Scripture that there is hope and restoration for any believer who truly repents.

This guide has been prepared to equip you to plan and lead a study of *When Godly People Do Ungodly Things* for groups in your church or community. You will find administrative guidance; help for planning and promoting the study, including plans for an optional retreat; and step-by-step instructions for conducting the group-study sessions.

COURSE OVERVIEW

This course was designed to be completed over seven weeks through a combination of daily, individual study and weekly group sessions.

INDIVIDUAL STUDY
Each participant needs a copy of *When Godly People Do Ungodly Things* member book, which contains reading assignments and activities designed to reinforce and apply learning. The member book is divided into an introduction and six weeks of content. Every week's material contains five daily lessons, each requiring about 45 minutes to complete. Participants complete the daily reading and the learning activities at home in preparation for the weekly group sessions.

GROUP SESSIONS
Participants meet once each week for a 1- to 1½-hour group session that guides them to discuss and apply what they have learned during their daily, individual study. Each session will include group discussion and a 30-minute video presentation in which Beth Moore enhances the material in the member book.

RESOURCES
These resources are available for leaders and participants.
• *When Godly People Do Ungodly Things Member Book* provides an introduction and six weeks of daily, bibli-cal studies to guide participants to authentic repentance and restoration. Order item 0-6330-9035-2
• *When Godly People Do Ungodly Things Leader Kit* contains one copy of the member book, this leader guide, and two DVDs that feature Beth Moore's teaching sessions and bonus discussion times on location in Jackson Hole, Wyoming. Order item 0-6330-9036-0
• *When Godly People Do Ungodly Things Leader Guide* Offers step-by-step suggestions for facilitating six group sessions using the member book and the DVDs. Also includes plans for an optional weekend retreat to launch your study. Order item 0-6330-9014-X
• *When Godly People Do Ungodly Things Audio CD Collection* Provides the audio portions of Beth Moore's video presentations on seven CDs. Listening guide included. Order item 0-6330-9029-8

You will also need the following:
• Registration tables
• Registration cards
• An attendance sheet
• Name tags and markers
• Bibles, pens, pencils
• A DVD player and monitor
• Tear sheets and markers

LEADERSHIP RESPONSIBILITIES
The leader should be someone who is interested in exploring the crucial truths of this course and who desires to help others grow in intimacy with God. A long list of qualifications and years of teaching experience are not required. A heart prepared by God—being available, teachable, and vulnerable—is more important. Paramount to this leader's success is a strong commitment to the study of this course and a faithful fulfillment of the basic responsibilities of group leadership.

Because of the nature of this study, small groups of no more than 10-12 people are encouraged. Each session is designed to encourage participants to discuss issues that are personal. Small groups allow more freedom to share openly. Stress from the beginning the need for confidentiality among group members. *When Godly People Do Ungodly Things* is a study designed to help believers find hope, healing, and restoration.

Leaders need to be responsible for—
- Providing administrative leadership for the group;
- Scheduling the study;
- Promoting the study and coordinating enrollment;
- Ordering and distributing resources;
- Maintaining and submitting records of participation each week as Discipleship Training attendance;
- Greeting and registering participants as they arrive at the introductory session;
- Checking members' attendance and homework prior to each week's meeting;
- Taking prayer requests, conducting a prayer time at the beginning of the session, praying for participants, and encouraging participants to pray for one another;
- Facilitating each group study session, following the suggestions provided in each session of this guide;
- Communicating with members periodically to offer help and to encourage them to complete their daily assignments in the member book;
- Promoting fellowship among group members;
- Noting opportunities for follow-up ministry.

ACCOUNTABILITY FOLLOW-UP
Some group members may need more accountability than just the seven weeks of group sessions. One thing to consider would be to form small accountability groups that would continue meeting after the study is over. If at all possible, form accountability groups for those interested before the end of this study. Encourage accountability groups to begin meeting immediately for continuity sake and so those involved will not become discouraged. Both week 6 of the study and the following list give practical guidelines for an ongoing accountability group.

Accountability Groups
1. Groups of no more than three persons meet weekly to hold each other accountable for spiritual transformation.
2. Set group goals. Meet weekly to go over the following:
   - Have you been a testimony this week to the greatness of Jesus Christ with both your words and actions?
   - Have you been exposed to sexually alluring material or allowed your mind to entertain inappropriate sexual thoughts about another this week?
   - Have you lacked integrity this week—by lying, financial misdealings, or coveting?
   - Have you been honoring, understanding and generous in your important relationships this week?
   - Have you damaged another person by your words, either behind their back or face-to-face?
   - Have you given in to any addictive behavior this week? Explain.

- Do you continue to be angry toward another?
- Have you secretly wished for the misfortune of another so that you might excel?
- Did you finish your reading/homework?
- Did you hear from God?
- What is He leading you to do?
- Add any others you wish …
- Have you been completely honest with me?[1]

3. Accountability groups should be established for three to six months. After that, reevaluate to see if changes need to be made or new groups formed.
4. Partners establish a common prayer list and pray for each other daily.
5. All information shared is strictly confidential.

FACILITATING DISCUSSION
You will find many applications in this study for a contemporary walk with God. Beth Moore applies many of the course's concepts in her video presentations. Also, the member book encourages participants to apply what they are learning as they complete their daily assignments.

One purpose of the small-group discussion each week is to enable members to make meaningful application to their daily lives. Small-group facilitators will guide discussions of each week's Principle Questions, listed at the beginning of each week's material in the member book, as well as the Personal Discussion Questions. Small-group facilitators can use the following guidelines to make these discussion times effective in challenging participants spiritually and in promoting life change.

- Arrange the chairs in the meeting room in a circle or a semicircle so that participants can see one another. Seating should not physically exclude anyone.
- Greet members as they arrive. Start the meeting on time. Allow 5 minutes for prayer requests; then pray or ask a participant to pray. Make notes when requests are shared. Assure members that you are concerned not only about their spiritual growth but also about their personal lives. Encourage them to pray for one another during the week. If someone is experiencing difficult circumstances, write a note or call between sessions to say that you are praying.
- Spend 20 minutes discussing the week's Principle Questions (listed at the beginning of each week's material in the member book) and 20 minutes discussing Personal Discussion Questions (designated by the apple symbol in the member book). Emphasize that only participants who wish to respond should do so; no one is required to share responses. Do not force the discussion questions on members. Adapt and change them as necessary.

Be flexible if members wish to spend more time on one group of questions or if they raise specific issues. Be sensitive to members' particular needs as the discussion progresses. Remember that your job is not to teach the material but to encourage and lead participants to share their insights about the work they did during the week and to apply the content to their spiritual journeys.

- Be personally involved without relinquishing leadership. A facilitator's role is that of a fellow disciple who shares the same struggles the other participants have in their spiritual lives. You need to be emotionally vulnerable and willing to share your feelings and responses. However, recognize that someone must lead the group and direct the discussion at all times. Be flexible, but do not allow the discussion to veer off on a tangent. Keep the focus on the week's content and its application.
- Create a relaxed atmosphere to help every member feel a sense of belonging. Use first names. Don't rush discussion.
- Pray for the Holy Spirit's leadership; then allow Him freedom to direct the session as He wills. His movement may be evident in tears of joy or conviction, emotional or spiritual brokenness, or the thrill of a newfound insight. Be sensitive to signs of God's work in a person's life and follow up by asking the person to share. Giving participants the opportunity to testify to what God is doing is very important. Often, the testimony may help another person with a similar issue. Follow the Holy Spirit's leadership as God works in these discussions.
- Be sure that you do not talk too much as facilitator. Do not be afraid of periods of silence.
- Be an encourager. Show a caring, loving spirit. Communicate your acceptance and concern, especially if your group includes non-Christians. Create an atmosphere that communicates, "I accept you as you are." Accepting participants does not necessarily mean that you agree with their values or choices. You can love a person without agreeing with her. If a participant shares something that makes her feel vulnerable or ashamed, say something like: "I know your sharing took a lot of courage. I admire you for being willing to share it."
- Listen intently and aggressively. When someone shares something personal or painful, lean toward her. Use facial expressions to show concern. Nod your head.
- Be ready to address special needs that members may reveal. If someone is unsaved, follow the Holy Spirit's leadership to know the right time to talk with the person privately to lead her to Christ. If a participant reveals emotional pain or family problems, assure her of the group's concern and support and pause briefly to

pray with the person. Then offer to meet with her later to help her find additional help if needed.
- Set boundaries. Don't permit a group member to act in a verbally abusive way toward another member. Do not force group members to do or say anything they are not willing to do or say. Try gently nudging a group member to a point of discovery and growth instead of pushing her to a conclusion for which she is not ready.
- Be enthusiastic!
- End the discussion period on time. You will face a challenge each week in bringing the discussion to an end in time for members to have a five-minute break before the large group reconvenes. At the first session emphasize the need to conclude on time each week. A few minutes before time to end the discussion period, help the person speaking reach a point of closure. Ask if anyone has anything to add. Allow response; then at some point end the discussion. If someone is not finished, affirm the importance of what the person is saying. Offer to continue the discussion next week and ask that member to introduce the topic at the beginning of the next meeting. Or you may need to spend time privately with the person if the topic does not relate to the entire group. Be sure you have tied loose ends. Did you put someone on hold during the discussion? Did you get back to the person? Was someone's sharing interrupted as you moved to focus on someone else's response? Did you reach closure with the original speaker? Finally, remind group members to pray for one another during the week.

COPING WITH PROBLEMS

No matter how meaningful the study and how effective the leadership, difficulties can arise. Following are common problems and suggestions for dealing with them.

Absenteeism. Absentees miss a potentially life-changing experience and diminish others' learning. If a participant is absent, contact the person, communicate your concern, and encourage her to make up the work. Otherwise, a participant will quickly get further behind and will likely drop out.

Not completing at-home assignments. Emphasize in the introductory session that a significant course requirement is doing daily study at home, including completion of the learning activities. State that each person's book will be checked before each session to see that homework was completed. Anyone unwilling to make this commitment should not participate in the study.

If someone has not completed the week's assignments, encourage the person to stay up-to-date to gain the greatest benefits from the study. If someone continually refuses to complete the assignments, meet with her and suggest that she withdraw and participate at a time when she can devote herself adequately to the study.

Disagreement with the content. Some debate in a group is productive. Remember that the Scriptures should always be the final source of authority. If debate becomes counterproductive, suggest that you and the participant discuss the matter later so that other members can participate in the present discussion.

Do not feel threatened if someone expects you to be an authority and to answer all of her questions. Emphasize your role as the facilitator of the discussion, pointing out that participants are to learn from one another and that you are not an authority on the subject. Suggest that a volunteer research the question during the week and report at the next meeting if the person insists that an answer is important to her.

A participant who dominates the group. Ways a person may dominate a group are—

• claiming a major portion of each discussion period to talk about her issues;

• repeatedly waiting until the last 10 minutes to introduce an emotionally charged story or problem;

• attempting to block other group members' sharing;

• judging others' behavior or confessions;

• challenging your leadership in a hostile way;

• criticizing other group members' motives or feelings.

As the facilitator, make sure every person has an opportunity to share. Discourage dominating members by calling on others, by asking someone to speak who has not yet responded, or by focusing directly on someone else. If these methods do not work, talk privately with the dominating person and enlist the person's support in involving everyone in future discussions.

When a person is going into too much detail and is losing the attention of the group, you will usually notice that the group has disconnected. Direct the sharing back on course by discreetly interrupting the person and by restating the point she is trying to make: "So what you are saying is …" Another method is to interrupt and restate the question you originally asked: "And Liz, what did you learn about God's love through that experience?" Even if the speaker is unsettled by this response, she should respond by restating the response more succinctly.

¹Neil Cole, *Cultivating a Life for God* (Carol Stream, IL: ChurchAmart Resources, 1999), 64.

ABOUT THE AUTHOR

Julie Woodruff, the writer of the leader guide, is an active women's ministry leader in her church and community. She currently leads a community-wide Bible study for women from 20 different churches and 8 denominations.

Julie began the women's ministry at West Conroe Baptist Church in Conroe, Texas, where her husband was the pastor for over 13 years. Julie also taught a women's Sunday School class and Bible study there.

Julie and her husband, Sid, reside in Hendersonville, Tennessee, with their two children, Lauren and Jordan.

CONDUCTING A RETREAT

Because of the nature of this study that deals with Satan's seductive power, it is important for participants to understand the importance of focusing on Jesus, the One who has the power to set us free. The purpose of this retreat is—

- to focus on God's power and ability to heal, restore, and sanctify us through and through;
- to proclaim that Jesus is Lord above all rulers, powers, kingdoms, and every pretension that sets itself up against the knowledge of God;
- to proclaim that we are "more than conquerors through [Christ]" (Rom. 8:37).

The following is a plan for conducting a retreat to launch the study of *When Godly People Do Ungodly Things*. Adjust these plans to fit your situation and needs.

ENLISTING LEADERS

Each coordinator may need a committee to support her assignments. Involving people in the planning raises interest. Having regular planning meetings to make sure everyone is on task or to see whether some areas need more resources is a great advantage to a successful retreat.

PRAYER COORDINATOR

Prayer will be the most important time spent in retreat preparation. Pray for God to lead you to individuals to serve on the retreat committee, for all details concerning the retreat, and for those who will participate.

- Choose a prayer committee of persons who are committed to praying.
- Before the retreat, pray for the planning details and each coordinator by name.
- Set up a prayer chain of prayer warriors who will not be attending to sign up for 15-minute increments to pray throughout the duration of the retreat.
- Equip the prayer warriors with specific prayer needs and Scripture to go with the request as well as the names of all participants and leaders.

RETREAT COORDINATOR

- Decide on the dates and location of the retreat. Suggestions include a retreat center, camp, lodge, or any location away from the distractions of everyday life.
- Choose and enlist small-group facilitators (preferably those who will lead small groups during the study) and

committee members who can fulfill their duties with servant hearts.

- Plan regular meetings with coordinators to discuss plans, to get updates on how each committee is progressing, and to make adjustments as necessary.
- Be available to all coordinators to help them accomplish their tasks and encourage them along the way.
- Once registration has been completed, divide the participants into small groups and assign each group a facilitator. Preferably, these will be the same groups that will participate in the study together.
- Pray for all facilitators and participants.
- Help other facilitators when they need assistance.
- Enlist persons to share testimonies at the retreat.
- Speak and lead at the retreat at designated times.

MUSIC COORDINATOR

- Provide music to exalt the Savior and invite worship.
- Enlist musicians.
- Make arrangements for sound equipment and power point if needed. Responsible for seeing that choruses, responsive reading, and anything else needed gets on power point.
- Suggested choruses found on Michael W. Smith, *Worship Again* album. Theme chorus suggestion: "Lord Have Mercy" 2000 Integrity's Hosanna! Music/ASCAP. Other chorus suggestions: "I Give You My Heart" and "There Is None Like You, You Are Holy (Prince of Peace)"

ADMINISTRATION COORDINATOR

- Work with the Retreat Coordinator to determine location and fee. Keep in mind the food and site expenses.
- Record decisions made at each planning meeting.
- Keep account of finances.
- Work with the Promotion Coordinator to conduct the registration for the retreat.
- Order *When Godly People Do Ungodly Things Member Book* for each participant. Include the cost of the workbook in the total cost of the retreat.

DECORATION COORDINATOR

- Use apples as decorations to coordinate with the cover of the workbook. Consider asking small-group leaders to hostess and decorate their table for dinner.
- Have Scripture taken from the study printed and hung around the meeting room.

- Make goodie bags or packets for each participant. Include schedule for the weekend, workbook, affirmation cards and anything else you would like to include such as pen, paper, candy, tissues, and so forth.

PROMOTION/GAMES COORDINATOR
- Promote the retreat with signs and announcements providing all necessary information.
- Work with the Administration Coordinator to conduct registration for the retreat.
- Choose icebreakers and games for group building.
- Provide small prizes for the puzzle contest.

FOOD ORGANIZER/HOSTESS
- Organizes and provides all food and serving items if food is not already provided at the retreat location.
- Plans and provides snacks for breaks. One idea is to use apples and apple cider or juice to coordinate with the art in the workbook.

MATERIALS COORDINATOR
- Make plenty of 3 x 5 affirmation cards and print Hebrews 10:25 at the bottom of each. You may decorate these if you like with apple stickers or stamps and tie them with raffia. Or they may be plain—the most important thing is what participants write, not the decoration! Place several cards in each packet.
- Procure enough manila envelopes for each participant to have one. Write each attendee's name on an envelope.
- Tape envelopes on the wall around the meeting room.
- Make copies needed for group activities, such as the personal devotion "Standing Together", "Partners in Prayer" worksheets, and responsive readings (pp. 14-15).
- Copy heart puzzles (p. 13) in enough colors for every small group to have a different color heart. Cut apart the puzzles, putting each into a zip bag or an envelope. Assign small-group leaders their color in advance.
- Trace puzzle onto cardboard for each small-group leader.
- Make a large cardboard heart so that leaders can attach completed puzzles to the large heart on the wall.
- Provide a small glue stick for each small-group leader.

RETREAT SCHEDULE

OPENING SESSION—FRIDAY EVENING
1. Dinner

2. Welcome

3. Make introductions. Give instructions for the weekend.

4. Explain that affirmation cards have been included in participants' packet. Encourage participants to write notes of encouragement to each member of her small group as well as others and place them in the envelope with the person's name on it. Before leaving the retreat, each person will receive her personal envelope.

5. At registration give each participant a puzzle piece in the color that corresponds to her small group. Ask each participant to write her name on the puzzle piece and find others who have the same color puzzle piece. Return to the small-group leaders any pieces not used. When groups are together, ask them to put their puzzle together, gluing the pieces on the cardboard heart. If there aren't enough in the group to finish the puzzle, the group leader will have the extra pieces and can finish the heart. The first group to complete the puzzle wins the prize. When every group has finished, recognize the winning group. (Give a simple prize to give each member of the group.) Have group leaders take their hearts and place them on the larger heart hanging on the wall.

6. Have someone read these Scriptures (also on p. 14):

   "The heart is deceitful above all things and beyond cure. Who can understand it? 'I the Lord search the heart and examine the mind, to reward a man according to his conduct, according to what his deeds deserve.' " "Heal me, O Lord, and I will be healed; save me and I will be saved, for you are the one I praise" (Jer. 17:9-10,14).

   "The heart is hopelessly dark and deceitful, a puzzle that no one can figure out. But I, GOD, search the heart and examine the mind. I get to the heart of the human. I get to the root of things. I treat them as they really are, not as they pretend to be. GOD, pick up the pieces. Put me back together again. You are my praise!" Jeremiah 17:9-10,14 (The Message).

7. Music: Suggested theme song, "Lord Have Mercy" (see under Music Coordinator)

8. Say to the group, *When Godly People Do Ungodly Things* is about God picking up and putting back together the pieces of broken hearts and lives of believers who have been seduced by the enemy and fallen into sin. This study is also a warning to strong believers to beware of the enemy's schemes and to stand firm.

9. Enlist someone to share a testimony about being seduced by Satan or share the following story.

> Pastor Jessie's story is fairly common. Upon completing Bible College, he entered ministry with a sincere desire to "walk in a manner pleasing to the Lord." At first, he maintained a healthy relationship with God, ministering to his flock out of the spiritual abundance that came from his vibrant devotional life. Eventually people began flocking to his church. This taste of success drove Jessie on. As his ever-increasing responsibilities demanded more of his time, his prayer life began to dwindle. When he did try to pray, heaven seemed closed to him. Rather than spending time in the Word seeking the spiritual nourishment he needed personally, he simply spent his time looking for sermon material. Over a period of months, the fountain of life had dried up for him. True, his ministry continued to flourish, but inwardly he was growing increasingly apathetic and cold hearted.
>
> Jessie didn't realize it, but his spiritual listlessness made him an open target for the enemy. During this period of time, he began having occasional lustful thoughts. At first, he would shut them out, but as time went on, he increasingly entertained them. One day, while on the Internet, the thought came to him to type a sexual phrase into the search engine. With a mounting curiosity and a depleted spiritual life, he gave in to the temptation ... he spent two hours rushing through dozens of adult websites. Jessie had just entered the dark realm of pornography.
>
> Over the next several months, this once-godly-man plunged deeper and deeper into the sewers of perverted images. He kept telling himself that he would quit, not realizing that every single visit to a porn site was digging him into a deeper pit that would be harder to climb out of. Getting caught by his wife was a beginning, but he had developed a serious addiction by this time."[1]

10. Pray

11. Give directions to the locations where small groups will meet. Explain that this will be the small group that they will be with the entire retreat. Dismiss to small group.

12. Small Groups: Read 1 Corinthians 10:1-13. Discuss the following questions (Discussion 1, p. 14).

   1. Based on Paul's declaration in verses 1-5, what did the Israelites count on to protect them from God's judgment? Did those things protect them? What do you look to as your guarantee from God's judgment?
   2. According to verses 6-10, what did the Israelites do that resulted in God's judgment?
   3. Are you susceptible to any of these things? If so, which ones?
   4. What does verse 12 tell us about thinking we've got our act together?
   5. What helps you keep temptations under control before they grow into sin?
   6. How can the promises in verse 13 help you in your spiritual battles?
   7. How can being in an accountability group help you stand up under temptations?

13. Prayer Partner: Ask each participant to pair up with another person to become a prayer partner. Give each person a "Partners in Prayer" sheet (p. 14). Ask them to fill out the information on their partner and then spend time praying for one another.

14. Break: Have snacks and a time of fellowship. You may plan guided games or give participants free time to fellowship with one another.

SATURDAY MORNING

1. Breakfast

2. Personal Devotion "Standing Together" (p. 14)

3. Worship: This is to be a celebration of praise. Ask participants to speak the names of the Lord that mean the most to them. Music Suggestion—"You Are Holy (Prince of Peace)" Upbeat praise songs

4. Enlist someone to share how she was encouraged by another believer during a time of battle in her life.

5. Divide into small groups. Ask a volunteer to read Ephesians 6:10-18. Discuss the following questions (Discussion 2, p. 15).
   1. From our Scripture reading about the armor of God, what battle does Paul see raging? What is it over?

2. List the six armor pieces. Which are offensive weapons? Which are defensive weapons?

3. What should our attitude be as we face forces of evil?

4. What part does prayer play in this battle?

5. If you compare your spiritual armor to this list, where are you strong? Weak? What are some things you need to do to prepare for battle?

6. What is at stake if you don't equip yourself for battle?

7. What evidence do you see of a battle raging in your life? What battles do you see being fought in your church, workplace, community, our nation, and the world? What would it mean for you to stand firm?

6. Form a circle, hold hands, and pray for courage to stand firm in the midst of battle.

7. Break

8. Return to small groups. Ask a volunteer to read Romans 8:28-39. Ask members the following questions for discussion (Discussion 3, p. 15).

   1. Do you see yourself more as an optimist or as a pessimist?

   2. What confidence does verse 28 give you about the events that occur in your life? Does this apply to times of suffering, difficulty, seduction?

   3. According to verses 29-30, what are four things that God has already done for a believer?

   4. How do verses 31-35 give confidence to a believer who is being persecuted or is guilty of having allowed Satan to seduce them?

   5. How could the things mentioned in verses 38-39 disrupt your trust in God's love?

   6. Have you ever experienced feelings of despair and loneliness when you felt separated from God? Describe how you felt.

9. Dismiss to Worship

10. Worship: Begin worship by reading Romans 8:28,31-35,37-39 either in unison or responsively. If read responsively, the worship leader reads the light print and the worshippers respond by reading the bold print. (Print handouts from p. 15.)

"We know that in all things God works for the good of those who love him, who have been called according to his purpose.

If God is for us, who can be against us?

He who did not spare his own Son, but gave him up for us all—how will he not also, along with him, graciously give us all things?

Who will bring any charge against those whom God has chosen? It is God who justifies.

Who is he that condemns? Christ Jesus, who died—more than that, who was raised to life—is at the right hand of God and is also interceding for us.

Who shall separate us from the love of Christ? Shall trouble or hardship or persecution or famine or nakedness or danger or sword?

No, in all these things we are more than conquerors through him who loved us.

For I am convinced that neither death nor life, neither angels nor demons, neither the present nor the future, nor any powers, neither height nor depth, nor anything else in all creation, will be able to separate us from the love of God that is in Christ Jesus our Lord."

---

11. Worship leader leads or sings praise music that speaks of God's love for us.

12. Ask the question, "What does it mean to you that you are more than a conqueror through Christ?" Ask participants to answer using a word to describe what it means to them. This is not meant to be a lengthy testimony, just say a word.

13. Continue time of praise music.

14. Retreat leader gives the closing challenge.

---

[1]Steve Gallagher, "Devastated by Internet Porn," Pure Life Ministries, 15 December 2000 [cited 5 February 2003]. Available from Internet: *www.purelifeministries.org/mensarticle1.htm.*

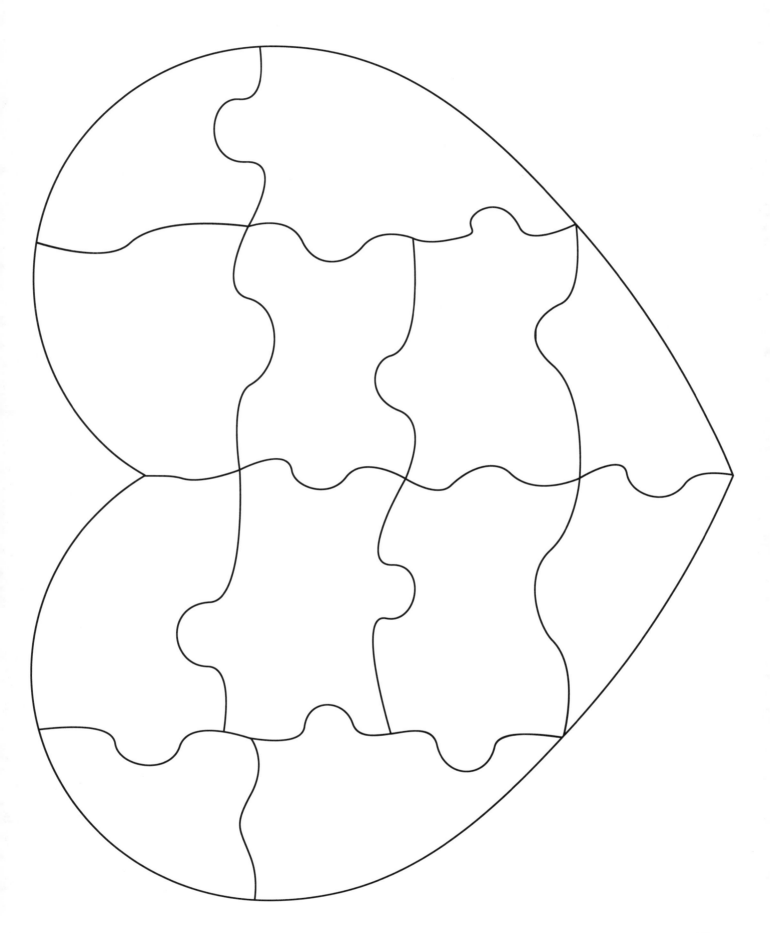

Jeremiah 17:9-10,14

"The heart is deceitful above all things and beyond cure. Who can understand it? 'I the Lord search the heart and examine the mind, to reward a man according to his conduct, according to what his deeds deserve.'" "Heal me, O Lord, and I will be healed; save me and I will be saved, for you are the one I praise."

Jeremiah 17:9-10,14

"The heart is hopelessly dark and deceitful, a puzzle that no one can figure out. But I, GOD, search the heart and examine the mind. I get to the heart of the human. I get to the root of things. I treat them as they really are, not as they pretend to be." "GOD, pick up the pieces. Put me back together again. You are my praise!"

(THE MESSAGE)

DISCUSSION I

1. Based on Paul's declaration in verses 1-5, what did the Israelites count on to protect them from God's judgment? Did those things protect them? What do you look to as your guarantee from God's judgment?
2. According to verses 6-10, what did the Israelites do that resulted in God's judgment?
3. Are you susceptible to any of these things? If so, which ones?
4. What does verse 12 tell us about thinking we've got our act together?
5. What helps you keep temptations under control before they grow into temptations and sin?
6. How can the promises in verse 13 help you in your spiritual battles?
7. How can being in an accountability group help you stand up under temptations?

PARTNERS IN PRAYER

1. Your prayer partner's name and phone number:

   _____

2. Share with each other about your backgrounds, vocation, families, and interests.

3. Share with each other personal prayer requests, fears or feelings about taking this study, anything that you desire to share that concerns this study. Record your partner's requests on the back.

4. Set a time each week you can call and pray with each other or think of a time each of you can pause to pray for the other each week: _____

5. Pause now and pray for each other.

STANDING TOGETHER

Read 1 Thessalonians 5:14-24.
Who is Paul speaking to in verse 14? _____

In verses 14-22, Paul lists 14 things that we as believers are to do for one another, what are they? *(Write down as many as you can on the back.)*

Based on this list, what are some personal areas that you need to work on?

How would you summarize the goal and hope of the Christian life in your own words (vv. 23-24)?

_____

Hebrews 10:25 says, "Let us not give up meeting together, as some are in the habit of doing, but let us encourage one another—and all the more as you see the Day approaching."

As believers we must stand together. Don't forget to write affirmation cards to your small group! Pray.

"We know that in all things God works for the good of those who love him, who have been called according to his purpose.

If God is for us, who can be against us?

He who did not spare his own Son, but gave him up for us all—how will he not also, along with him, graciously give us all things?

Who will bring any charge against those whom God has chosen? It is God who justifies.

Who is he that condemns? Christ Jesus, who died—more than that, who was raised to life—is at the right hand of God and is also interceding for us.

Who shall separate us from the love of Christ? Shall trouble or hardship or persecution or famine or nakedness or danger or sword?

No, in all these things we are more than conquerors through him who loved us.

For I am convinced that neither death nor life, neither angels nor demons, neither the present nor the future, nor any powers, neither height nor depth, nor anything else in all creation, will be able to separate us from the love of God that is in Christ Jesus our Lord."

ROMANS 8:28,31-35,37-39 (THE MESSAGE)

DISCUSSION 2

1. From our Scripture reading about the armor of God, what battle does Paul see raging? What is it over?
2. List the six armor pieces. Which are offensive weapons? Which are defensive weapons?
3. What should our attitude be as we face forces of evil?
4. What part does prayer play in this battle?
5. If you compare your spiritual armor to this list, where are you strong? Weak? What are some things you need to do to prepare for battle?
6. What is at stake if you don't equip yourself for battle?
7. What evidence do you see of a battle raging in your life? What battles do you see being fought in your church, workplace, community, our nation, and the world? What would it mean for you to stand firm?

DISCUSSION 3

1. Do you see yourself more as an optimist or as a pessimist?

2. What confidence does verse 28 give you about the events that occur in your life? Does this apply to times of suffering, difficulty, seduction?

3. According to verses 29-30, what are four things that God has already done for a believer?

4. How do verses 31-35 give confidence to a believer who is being persecuted or is guilty of having allowed Satan to seduce them?

5. How could the things mentioned in verses 38-39 disrupt your trust in God's love?

6. Have you ever experienced feelings of despair and loneliness when you felt separated from God? Describe how you felt.

INTRODUCTORY SESSION

BEFORE THE SESSION:

1. Spend time praying for your group although you might not even know their names yet. Ask God for sensitivity to those that He will assign to your group. Being faithful to pray not only before the study but throughout the study is a must. This study will be difficult for many people—maybe even yourself—because of its nature. However, nothing is too difficult for God. Enjoy the sweet time of fellowship with Him as you prepare to lead. As you pray for your group, you will be blessed to watch God work among you. Ask God to give you a supernatural love for each member of your group. By the time they arrive, your heart will already be tendered toward them.

2. Provide markers and materials for making name tags for all persons attending.

3. Plan to have workbooks available for purchase.

4. Prepare a "Getting to Know You" sheet that each participant will fill out. This sheet will provide you with information about them. Include a place for name, address, phone number, and email address, but also ask questions that will help you get to know the person. The more you know, the better equipped you will be to minister to needs of group members.

5. Provide paper for participants to use in a group activity.

6. Arrange to have a DVD player and monitor for the video presentation.

DURING THE SESSION:

1. Play praise music while participants arrive. As persons arrive, introduce yourself and direct them to the nametags. Ask them to fill out the "Getting to Know You" sheet while waiting for everyone to arrive (see p. 31). Have them return completed sheets to you.

2. Welcome participants and introduce yourself. Your excitement as the leader will be contagious. You may want to create an icebreaker for participants to get to know one another.

3. Tell the group that you have been praying for them. This introductory session is a great time to lay a foundation for people to share with one another, to get comfortable with each other, and to establish a common goal and purpose. One way to establish a common goal or purpose is by asking each participant what led them to this particular study. Always remember that some will be fearful of sharing openly in front of a group. Express sensitivity to that and alleviate fear by expressing that everyone is encouraged to share, but no one will ever be forced to share. Even the shy person can be brought into discussion by asking general, non-threatening questions.

4. Pass out member books and ask members to scan the first week's daily assignments. Explain that they are to complete a week of study before each group session. Encourage them to complete each week's assignment for the most benefit. Emphasize that although the daily assignments are crucial, members should attend the weekly sessions even if their work is incomplete.

5. Give instructions and information about the course. Include the following points.
   a. Emphasize the primary purposes of small-group discussion are—
      • accountability. In-depth Bible studies are most often completed successfully in a group.
      • to underscore basic biblical truths. This will be accomplished through discussing answers to the Principle Questions, which ensure that the week's content has been received and understood.
      • to personally apply the study. Application will be accomplished through discussing answers to the Personal Discussion Questions.
   b. Express the need to be good stewards of time. Ask members to adopt these time guidelines.
      • Leaders: Be early each week!
      • Members: Be on time each week!
      • Small groups: Start on time! Leaders must start on time regardless of the number present.

6. View the video presentation.

7. Pass out strips of paper to each person. Ask group members to write down a prayer request for themselves, something they hope to receive from participating in this study. Fold them and pass them to the leader without names on them. The leader will read the requests and pray for group members.

AFTER THE SESSION

1. Read through each "Getting to Know You" sheet and learn as much as you can about group members. Memorize their names and pray for each person.

Video Response Sheet

INTRODUCTORY GROUP SESSION

IN THE BEGINNING...

1. We are the _____reason_____ there was ever a _____beginning_____.

2. We were _____created_____ out of the ___Holy___ ___Us___ of God.

3. We were created out of _____fellowship_____, for _____fellowship_____.

4. LORD God is the _____covenant_____ name of God.

5. Man was created from the _____touch_____ of God.

6. We are made to _____join_____ God in the garden that He has _____planted_____ for us,

   and we are not _____satisfied_____ till we do.

7. All _____rebellion_____ begins with "I will." All _____obedience_____ to God begins with "Thy will."

8. _____Seduction_____ exists because we are the _____people_____ of God.

9. " 'Whoever touches ___you___ touches the _____apple_____ of His eye' " (Zech. 2:8).

10. The only _____reason_____ for our war is that we are the _____beloved_____ of God.

Session One

THE WARNING

BEFORE THE SESSION:

1. Pray for group members and yourself.
2. Write 2 Corinthians 11:2-3 from *The Amplified Bible* on a poster. Mount it on the wall for the whole study.

> "For I am zealous for you with a godly eager-ness and a divine jealousy, for I have betrothed you to one Husband, to present you as a chaste virgin to Christ. But [now] I am fearful, lest that even as the serpent beguiled Eve by his cun-ning, so your minds may be corrupted and seduced from wholehearted and sincere and pure devotion to Christ" (2 Cor. 11:2-3).

3. Provide markers, tear sheets, and paper.
4. Photocopy the Common Claims of the Seduced and cut into strips.*
5. Arrange to have a DVD player and monitor for the video presentation.

DURING THE SESSION:

1. Welcome group members by name as they arrive.
2. Show the video presentation.
3. Ask a volunteer to read Ephesians 6:10-18. Point out that the only two offensive weapons listed are the sword of the Spirit and prayer. Share with participants that throughout the course of this study, you will all be in a battle because the enemy hates the truth about him to be made known. However, you will learn how to fight the enemy with the sword and with prayer. Pray Ephesians 1:18-23 for the group. As you pray verse 18, "I pray also that the eyes of your heart may be enlight-ened," replace "your," with members' names.
4. Ask, "Why do you think Satan may be more active today in attacking Christians than ever before?" List responses on the board or tear sheet. What were the three streams of evidence you studied this week?
5. Ask a volunteer to read 2 Timothy 3:1-5. As the Scrip-ture is read, list on a tear sheet the descriptions Paul gives of people in the last days. Next, list ways you see the relevancy of these Scriptures today.
6. Divide into triads. Give each group the following assignment: Using the markers and paper provided, illustrate 1 Peter 5:8-9 by a drawing, poem, song, car-toon, or any way they choose. After five minutes, share the results with the entire group.
7. Discuss as a group the question on page 20, "Based on 1 Corinthians 6:18-20, why is sexual sin a perfect choice to achieve Satan's goals?"
8. Ask members to pair up. Give each pair an equal num-ber of strips with the common claims of the seduced. Ask pairs to describe the claims they have been given. Make a master list of common claims on a tear sheet, numbering them as they are discussed. After the dis-cussion, give each participant a slip of blank paper. Take a poll—have them list on their paper the number beside those they have personally experienced. Take these up without names. When all slips have been handed in, place a mark on the master list by each common claim that a group member has struggled with. This will encourage members who have been seduced to know that they are not alone.
9. Close the session in prayer.

Common Claims of the Seduced

1. Individuals reported that they were caught off guard by a sudden onslaught of temptation or attack.
2. The season of overwhelming temptation and seduc-tion often followed huge spiritual markers with God.
3. Everyone described a mental bombardment.
4. Many of those caught in relational seductions (not all seductions are relational) testified that Satan got to them through someone close by.
5. Many testified to early warning signals.
6. Many described their sudden behavioral patterns as totally uncharacteristic.
7. Virtually all of them described feelings and practices of isolation.
8. Without exception, deception and some level of secrecy were involved.
9. Many described overwhelming feelings of powerlessness.
10. Many described something we'll call an addictive nature to the seductive sin.
11. Most utterly hated what they were doing.
12. The seduction lasted only for a season.
13. Many describe a period of a spiritual numbness of sorts.
14. Many used the same peculiar word to describe what they had experienced.
15. Many describe the aftermath as a time of slowly increasing awareness rather than an instant wake up.
16. Feelings of devastation and indescribable sorrow finally came, ushering in deep repentance.

Video Response Sheet
GROUP SESSION I

1. There are _____ *many* _____ kinds of seduction.

2. Warfare is _____ *hardball* _____. Seduction is _____ *curveball* _____.

3. We can be _____ *sincere* _____, _____ *pure* _____, and wholeheartedly _____ *devoted* _____

   to God and be _____ *seduced* _____ by the serpent's cunning.

4. _____ *Never* _____ turn your _____ *back* _____ on the enemy.

   FOUR CLASSIC ASSAULTS OF THE ENEMY

   A. _____ *Doubt* _____

      God's counteroffer is _____ *faith* _____.

   B. _____ *Shame* _____

      God's counteroffer: Shame is not of _____ *Christ* _____.

   C. _____ *Fear* _____

      God's Counteroffer: He did not give us a _____ *spirit* _____ of fear.

   D. _____ *Blame* _____

      God's counteroffer: The _____ *peace* _____ of His authority.

5. The next generation is tired of _____ *hypocrisy* _____. They want to see _____ *authenticity* _____.

6. God knows where _____ *responsibility* _____ lies. _____ *responsibility* *We* _____ must take responsibility for our sin.

7. We get into a seductive mess by believing a _____ *responsibility* *lie* _____.

8. Our ticket to freedom is to look up with an unveiled face before God and say, "_____ *Heal* _____ *me* _____."

Session Two

GOD'S PERMISSIVE WILL

BEFORE THE SESSION:

1. Pray for each group member. Perhaps you have noticed someone struggling. Write that person a note or call to encourage her.
2. Make five placards with the following words on them: 1. Ignorance, 2. Spiritual passion that exceeds biblical knowledge, 3. Lack of discernment, 4. A lack of self-discernment, 5. Exposure to or experience with false worship or depravity in the past.
Hang them around the room.
3. Photocopy story excerpts from activity 6 for each member.*
4. Arrange to have a DVD player and monitor.

DURING THE SESSION:

1. Ask group members to share one thing they found encouraging in this week's homework. Give each person a slip of paper and have them write down their prayer request. Place all requests in a basket and then pass the basket around and have each group member draw one. Have a time of silent prayer. Ask everyone to pray for the request on the slip they received. Ask them also to pray for the session today.
2. View the video presentation.
3. Number off from 1-5. Have each group stand in front of the placard with the corresponding number. Each group is to come up with a skit to depict the weakness listed on their placard. Give the groups seven minutes to write their skit. After seven minutes, call for work to stop and watch as each group performs their skit. Discuss as a group how our weaknesses and areas of ignorance are huge vulnerabilities.
4. Discuss as a group the difference between willful and inadvertent sins.
5. Ask, "How do you think billboards, magazine covers, television shows, commercials, movies, or songs make us susceptible to seduction?" What are some ways that Satan can use our pasts against us?
6. Hand out the excerpts from real life stories and ask group members to underline the weakness or vulnerability that led to seduction. After participants have completed underlining, discuss as a group.

"So what if I was molested as a child. It's never bothered me before."

"I never knew my father. He bailed on us and ran off with a 17-year-old when I was 3 years old. I don't care. I never give the lousy excuse-for-a-man a second thought."

"My mom had me dancing in a topless joint for money when I was still a minor. Some kind of mom, huh? I just try never to think about it."

"I watched my father beat my mother nearly to death. He was the meanest drunk you can imagine. I'm never gonna be like him. In fact, I don't even think I'll ever get married."

"My dad was a pastor. We used to have to sit on the front row every Sunday and listen to him bang the pulpit, condemning the congregation for their horrible sins. You should have seen him at home. He made me sick."

"My sister died of cancer when she was nine and I was five. Our family never got over it. I don't remember a single sound of laughter in our house."

"My brother and I were in a fire when we were little boys. He burned to death. I've still got scars, but I go on living. You just can't let those kinds of things get to you."

7. Ask a volunteer to read Ephesians 6:10-13 from *The Amplified Bible* on pages 43-44 in the member book. Review these questions: What admonition does Paul give in these verses? Why are we to put on the armor of God? What are we not wrestling with? List the things we do wrestle with.
8. Divide the group into two groups. One group is Job. The other group is Peter. Each group's assignment is to summarize how their assigned man was attacked by Satan and for what purpose. What can we learn from their examples? Discuss with the entire group.
9. Close in prayer.

Video Response Sheet
GROUP SESSION 2

1. God is ever after proving us _____*genuine*_____.

2. As the latter days approach:

   A. The enemy is _____*furious*_____.

   B. God _____*wants*_____ to get the _____*bride*_____ ready.

3. Some things can only occur in your life through _____*warfare*_____.

4. God will never allow the enemy to sift any _____*believer*_____ that does not need something _____*sifted*_____.

5. God is after turning us inside out to put truth in our _____*inmost*_____ _____*parts*_____.

6. Satan hates anyone who learns to be _____*offensive*_____ with the sword of the Spirit.

7. Instead of _____*keeping*_____ your monster down, let God _____*deal*_____ with it.

8. God's Word applies to our _____*biggest*_____ _____*problems*_____.

Session Three

THE WATCHMAN

BEFORE THE SESSION:

1. Pray for group members and call any absentees.
2. Secure markers, tear sheets, marker board, and paper for group assignments.
3. Obtain a CD player and praise CD for the last activity.
4. Make copies of the three case studies.*
5. Arrange to have a DVD player and monitor.

DURING THE SESSION:

1. Ask for volunteers to recite 1 Thessalonians 5:23-24 from memory. Write the verse on a marker board and say it together, erasing a word each time you repeat it. Ask group members to pray this prayer in pairs, inserting their partner's name in the verse instead of "you."
2. View the video.
3. Divide group into triads. Give each group a marker and tear sheet and three minutes to complete the assignment—to list reasons to be happy in our faith. After three minutes, have each group share.
4. Ask for volunteers to share testimonies of praying unceasingly. Remind members that praying unceasingly means constant communication throughout the day and can take on many different forms. Ask, "What are some ways to pray unceasingly?"
5. Give each person a sheet of paper. Ask them to write down as many things as they can think of for which they are thankful. After two minutes collect the lists and read each to the group without using names. Celebrate God's goodness together.
6. Ask for volunteers to share testimonies from pages 60-61 in the member book.
7. Divide into three groups. Give each group one of the following case studies:

Case Study 1

Tom, a Christian churchgoing man, views what he calls light pornography and keeps a stack in his bathroom. No big deal. It's not the bad stuff. His wife doesn't like it, but he's done it since college. They've been married for years, and he has never been (physically) unfaithful. It hasn't caused him a problem.

What groundwork has Satan already laid in this situation? What is Tom's false sense of security?

Case Study 2

Sally struggles with homosexual tendencies and wants to be different and free from guilt. She attended a youth rally. The speaker hit hard on the sin of homosexuality. Feeling convicted and devastated by her sin, she received Christ and vowed never to return to her former practices.

She did her best to forget. Thinking normal must mean being married, she marries as quickly as she can. She struggles, but who doesn't? The problem is only in her imagination; no one knows her thoughts about the past. She hates it but doesn't know how to fix it. She tries to be good; she gets involved at church and tries to stay busy. Then one day a woman joins her prayer group. Not just any woman. A woman in active bondage to homosexual sin.

What groundwork has Satan already laid in this situation? What is Sally's false sense of security?

Case Study 3

A ministry bookkeeper, Ann borrows and repays the bank account for years. No one knows because she does the books. She pays it back anyway—eventually. She's gotten a little sloppy lately; the books are a tad behind. She'll catch up, though. Money is tight at home and she has a few outstanding debts, but the ministry has plenty. They'll never miss it. It's not a big deal. It's gone on for years.

It's not fair. Her husband left her with two teenagers and refuses to pay support. She just needs help till the courts get the whole mess straightened out. No one cares. No one knows. She'll pay it back. She's done it before.

What groundwork has Satan already laid in this situation? What is Ann's false sense of security?

8. Read Ephesians 4:30 and discuss as a group how we can grieve the Holy Spirit.
9. If you are not viewing the video, discuss the diagram on page 66. Fill in each part of the diagram and discuss it as a group. Share ways we can fortify our lives.
10. Close with worship. Ask volunteers to share testimonies of personal worship experiences this week. Listen to a favorite praise song. One suggestion is, "You are Holy" from Michael W. Smith's CD, "Worship Again." End with each person saying a one-sentence prayer that begins with "I praise You because …"

*Publisher grants permission to photocopy the case studies to be used in your small-group time.

Video Response Sheet
GROUP SESSION 3

1. We are the _____ *temple* _____ of the Holy Spirit.

2. Walls can represent being _____ *penned* _____ in or _____ *constricted* _____ or they can represent _____ *freedom* _____.

3. Some people fall into _____ *seduction* _____ because of _____ *spiritual* _____ *boredom* _____.

4. Satan knows that we were _____ *birthed* _____ to _____ *live* _____ and rebirthed to live _____ *more* _____ *abundantly* _____.

5. There is a _____ *danger* _____ *zone* _____ outside the walls.

6. We become so focused on what we _____ *should* _____ *not* _____ *do* _____ that we miss what we _____ *can* _____ *do* _____.

7. There are _____ *rivers* _____ of _____ *delight* _____.

8. The walls around us are the walls of the _____ *fire* _____ of God and His _____ *glory* _____ dwells within.

Session Four

WISE UP!

BEFORE THE SESSION:

1. Pray for group members and yourself. Send a note to those you sense may be struggling.
2. Provide cards for members' prayer requests.
3. Make copies of the True-False test for activity 1.*
4. Copy assignments for activity 7 on index cards.
5. Bring a rope, sentence strips, and tape for activity 8. Also cut out a large cardboard cross for the same activity.
6. Make two posters with the following definitions: Discernment: the ability to see through the masks Accountability: inviting others to see through us

DURING THE SESSION:

1. As members arrive, ask them to take the following True-False test, rewording false statements to make them true.

_____ Seduction always involves personal relationships between people.
_____ All unhealthy relationships are demonic seductions.
_____ Relationships aren't breeding grounds for seductions.
_____ Relational seduction always involves physical or sexual impropriety.

After everyone has completed the test, discuss how to reword the false statements to make them true. These statements can be found on page 79 of the member book.

1. Pass out prayer-request cards. Ask members to write their request on a card and exchange with another group member. Spend time in silent prayer as group members pray for the request they have been given.
2. View the video presentation.
3. Ask a volunteer to read Matthew 24:12 and discuss as a group the question on page 80, "What evidence can you see of hearts growing cold in our world today?"
4. Divide into groups of four. Each group assignment is to discuss the questions on page 81 in the member book. What might be the difference between a godly relationship and a spiritual relationship? Ask for volunteers in the small groups to share in a very general way—and certainly not using names—about a spiritual relationship that was not godly. Evaluate from each testimony what characteristics of the spiritual

relationship made it look appealing. After a few minutes of discussion, have small groups share characteristics with the entire group.

5. List on a tear sheet or marker board ways that Satan disguises himself.
6. As a group, define *sanctification*. Write the definition on a tear sheet and hang it on the wall. Discuss ways to sanctify ourselves.
7. Divide members into two groups.

   Group 1: Read Hebrews 4:12-13. List everything God's Word does.

   Group 2: Read Hebrews 4:14-16 and answer the following questions: Who is our High Priest? How does He relate to us? How are believers to respond? Share responses with the entire group.

8. Hand out strips of paper to group members and have them write down a word or sin that describes an entangling relationship. Ask for two volunteers to create the visual in this week's study. Have them stand side by side, and wrap a rope around both of them. Then ask group members to come and share their word, taping the descriptive word to the rope or on the volunteers! After all words have been taped to the persons, have them get out of the tangled mess. After they are free, ask them to hold the cardboard cross in between them. Discuss what happens when Christ stands between relationships. Give a round of applause for the volunteers as they are seated.
9. Ask a volunteer to read Philippians 2:15-16. Have participants work in pairs to paraphrase Paul's words in their own language.
10. Ask a volunteer to read Hebrews 10:24-25. Make a list of ways to fortify ourselves as we see the day approaching.
11. Call attention to the definitions of *Discernment* and *Accountability* hanging on the wall. According to this week's homework, define what it means to develop and practice godly discernment from a broader base and to develop and practice deliberate accountability from a narrower base (Member Book, p. 96).
12. Close in prayer asking God to give group members both discernment and accountability.

Video Response Sheet

GROUP SESSION 4

1. The Day approaching represents the day of _____Christ's_____ _____return_____.

2. Toward end times there will be increases in _____depravity_____, _____deception_____, and _____strongholds_____.

3. Toward end times there will also be an unparalleled _____outpouring_____ of the Holy Spirit.

4. Satan knows we will need _____one_____ _____another_____ more and more as the Day approaches.

5. Satan is doing everything he can to _____pervert_____ and _____destroy_____ relationships.

   Koinonia means _____fellowship_____. In its concept it also often infers _____impartation_____.

6. In any level of fellowship we are _____receiving_____ and _____giving_____ impartation.

7. True *koinonia* means good deposits.

8. We must _____purposely_____ develop smart hearts.

9. We are never told to love _____blindly_____.

10. We are told to love with

    • _____knowledge_____

    • depth of _____insight_____

    • and _____discernment_____

11. To _____live_____ well is to _____love_____ well.

12. Many of us want to _____minister_____ the Gospel without allowing it to be _____ministered_____ to us.

    The Greek word for "poor" is _____ptochos_____ which means "subsisting on the alms from others."

13. Our fellowship with _____one_____ _____another_____ begins with our fellowship with _____God_____.

14. Loving well is always _____deliberate_____.

THE WAY HOME

BEFORE THE SESSION:

1. Pray for group members and make contact with any who have been absent.

2. Provide index cards for group assignments.

3. Type, write, or photocopy the following five facts of restoration given this week in 1 Samuel 12:20-22. Make a copy for each group member.

> "Do not be afraid"
> "You have done all this evil"
> "Yet do not turn away from the LORD"
> "Serve the LORD with all your heart"
> "The LORD was pleased to make you his own."
> —1 Samuel 12:20-22

4. List the five facts of restoration down the side of a tear sheet. At the top, write "Difficult," Then draw a line, and write "Easy" on the other side of the line. Provide several markers for members to use and tape to hang the tear sheet on the wall.

DURING THE SESSION

1. Begin the session with a time of praise and thanksgiving.

2. View the video presentation.

3. Take a vote to see if group members believe that it is possible to be Had. Ask group members to share testimonies about times that they have been Had. Please be very general. The ground rule for sharing is that you don't share anything that you would be embarrassed tomorrow that you shared.

4. Divide into two groups. Ask each group to make a list of ways to help those who have been Had to heal. Share the lists with the entire group.

5. Discuss as a group what John the Baptist meant when he said, " 'Produce fruit in keeping with repentance' " (Matt. 3:8).

6. Ask a volunteer to read 1 Samuel 12:12-25. Have group members pair up and answer the question, "What do you think might be some ways that we switch our primary devotions to the visible princes of the earth?" After a short period of discussion, share some of the possible ways with the entire group.

7. List on a marker board the three primary areas the enemy can fuel fear in a Had. Divide into three groups and assign a fear to each group. Each group is to take the fear that they have been assigned and give examples of ways the enemy can use these fears in the life of a Had. Share examples with the large group and ask other group members to give input.

8. Based on the homework in day 4, ask the group to outline an action plan for dealing with fear. Include things to do and not to do, as well as Scripture that applies. Once a master plan is made, give out index cards and have group members copy the plan on a card. Encourage them to keep their index card handy so that when fear begins to manifest itself, they can be reminded that they are not to be afraid and that they can claim God's Word over their fears.

9. Give each group member a copy of the five facts about restoration from 1 Samuel 12:20-22. Ask them to underline the ones that are difficult and circle those that are easy for them to accept. Tally the results by having group members go to the tear sheet hanging on the wall and place a mark by each fact under "Difficult" or "Easy" just to see where the differences and similarities are in dealing with these five facts about restoration. They can all come at once and take turns tallying. That will take some of the pressure off of those who are quiet, and they may feel less intimidated because no one pays attention to what others mark. Discuss the results and pray for the entire group to have the courage to follow God's Word and plan for restoration.

10. Encourage members to be back for the last session. If you want to plan a time of fellowship for the last week, ask for volunteers to assist you.

Video Response Sheet

GROUP SESSION 5

1. The body of Christ must grow in _____ *discernment* _____.

2. We oftentimes _____ *rationalize* _____ what would be the right thing to do.

3. Sometimes we _____ *manipulate* _____ a wrong to try to make it right.

4. We must learn to _____ *admit* _____ we made a _____ *mistake* _____.

      QUESTIONS OF A HAD

      A. How could I do anything so _____ *stupid* _____?

      B. How can I _____ *forgive* _____ myself?

5. There is healing in _____ *understanding* _____.

      The Greek word for "understand" is *suniemi* which means "assembling individual _____ *facts* _____

      into an organized whole, as collecting the _____ *pieces* _____ of a _____ *puzzle* _____ and

      putting them together."

6. If we would _____ *receive* _____, _____ *accept* _____, and

      _____ *apply* _____ the forgiveness of God, that would cover our need to forgive ourselves.

      The original Greek for "forgiving, forgave" is _____ *charizomai* _____ which comes from *charis,*

      meaning "_____ *grace* _____."

7. _____ *Grace* _____ them as you have been _____ *graced* _____.

8. We have to allow _____ *God* _____ to take our horrible experience and _____ *baptize* _____

      it in a river of _____ *mercy* _____.

Session Six

SAFE IN HIS EMBRACE

BEFORE THE SESSION:

1. Pray for all group members. By now you know them well enough to know some of their specific needs. Call and encourage those who are struggling.
2. Arrange to have DVD player and monitor available. Notice that the video is not shown until the end in this session.
3. If you have planned for a time of celebration this week, make sure arrangements have been made for simple decorations, snacks, beverages, utensils, and so forth. A little food for thought: maybe you want to go all out with a feast to welcome some prodigal home!
4. Write assignments for activity 5 on index cards.

DURING THE SESSION:

1. Share testimonies of what God has revealed and taught group members through this study. Go around the circle and allow each member to participate by saying a sentence or more as the Holy Spirit leads. Celebrate His faithfulness and goodness.
2. Have group members pair up with another member, share prayer requests, and intercede in prayer on behalf of their partner.
3. Discuss as a group why detoxification, deprogramming, and reprogramming are important to the restoration process.
4. Ask the group to list the five facts about the conscience they learned this week.

    1. People with a guilty past can still enjoy a clear conscience.
    2. Good deeds cannot accomplish a clear conscience.
    3. The Holy Spirit works with the believer's conscience.
    4. The conscience is an indicator, not a transformer.
    5. The conscience can be seared.

As they are listed, write them on a tear sheet or marker board on the wall. Ask a volunteer to read 2 Corinthians 1:12. Based on this Scripture, define a clean conscience biblically and write the definition after the list of facts.

5. Divide into two groups. Give each group one of the following assignments:

Group 1: Explain how a believer can pursue and practice the sincere and sanctified life in the world.

Group 2: Explain how believers can pursue and practice the sanctified life in our relationships with other Christians.

6. Using the biblical steps to a fresh, clean conscience presented in day 4, ask group members which of those steps seems most difficult and why.

    1. Believe what God has already done for you.
    2. Go into the Holy of Holies without delay, and take your heavy conscience.
    3. Approach God with absolute sincerity and repentance.
    4. Now, ask God to cleanse your conscience just as His Word says.
    5. Approach God with a full assurance of faith.
    6. Record every bit of this process over the old tape.
    7. When possible and appropriate, make amends or restitution.

7. Ask a volunteer to read Luke 15:11-32. Discuss ways that we have all been like the prodigal son.
8. View the video.
9. Celebrate!

Video Response Sheet

GROUP SESSION 6

The Greek word for "understand" is *suniemi* which means "assembling individual facts into an organized whole, as collecting the pieces of a puzzle and putting them together."

Any eye that may be willing to be opened, any ear that might be willing to hear, any mind that might be willing to receive understanding could receive a puzzle piece and know just a measure of healing. So, Beloved, this is your piece. This is your joy.

1. The sin that is _____*different*_____ from ours always seems _____*worse*_____.

2. The Word of God _____*never*_____ teaches us to _____*break*_____ fellowship with the repentant.

3. We _____*cannot*_____ go on in our sin. The Holy Spirit will _____*convict*_____ us.

4. How do we go on from here? We go on _____*blessed*_____.

5. A true, _____*healed*_____ Had is so scared of herself that she will never live anywhere but _____*before*_____ the _____*face*_____ of God.

HOW TO USE THE DVDS

With the optional "Talk Times with Beth" on the DVDs, you are invited to join Beth Moore and the small group discussions that occurred after each session was taped in Jackson Hole, Wyoming.

Both DVDs included in the leader kit contain bonus material that can be used to enhance your group's study. After each of the teaching sessions, Beth led the group in a discussion time. With the ladies' permissions, those discussions were taped and edited for your potential use.

Including these discussions in your group study is optional, but you may find them beneficial. The bonus segment for each session runs around 7-8 minutes. To maximize the space available on the DVD discs, the bonus material for the Introductory Session has been placed on Disc 1. The other discussion times appear on Disc 2. You can access them through the main menu.

Suggestions for Using the DVDs

1. As part of your group's discussion time, show the bonus segment for that session.
2. Lengthen your session time to 90 minutes to allow more time for discussion. After viewing Beth's teaching session, follow the guidance suggested for group processing. Then start the additional 30 minutes by showing the bonus segment to spark more discussion.
3. Consider adding additional sessions to the study with the bonus segment used as the discussion starters. Facilitators will want to view these in advance and let the Holy Spirit direct the session as He wills.

    Review "Facilitating Discussion" beginning on page 5 of this guide. Work with your fellow disciples to apply God's truths to your lives.
4. Loan the DVDs disc to individuals for personal use.

DVD CHECKOUT

Participant	Borrowed	Returned	Participant	Borrowed	Returned
Sally Adams	DVD 1	✓			

ATTENDANCE

Participant	Intro.	1	2	3	4	5	6

Getting to Know You

Name _____

Address _____

Phone Number _____

E-mail _____

What led you to this study?

_____

What would you most like to get from this class?

_____

_____

It would be my privilege to pray for you during our time of study together. What one prayer request would you most like for me to bring before God?

_____

_____

Facilitator's name _____

Getting to Know You

Name _____

Address _____

Phone Number _____

E-mail _____

What led you to this study?

_____

What would you most like to get from this class?

_____

_____

It would be my privilege to pray for you during our time of study together. What one prayer request would you most like for me to bring before God?

_____

_____

Facilitator's name _____

Getting to Know You

Name _____

Address _____

Phone Number _____

E-mail _____

What led you to this study?

_____

What would you most like to get from this class?

_____

_____

It would be my privilege to pray for you during our time of study together. What one prayer request would you most like for me to bring before God?

_____

_____

Facilitator's name _____

Getting to Know You

Name _____

Address _____

Phone Number _____

E-mail _____

What led you to this study?

_____

What would you most like to get from this class?

_____

_____

It would be my privilege to pray for you during our time of study together. What one prayer request would you most like for me to bring before God?

_____

_____

Facilitator's name _____